mel bay presents

Understanding Guitar Chords

by Bob Balsley

CONTENTS

Visit us on the Web at http://www.melbay.com — E-mail us at email@melbay.com

INTRODUCTION

You've heard folkies strumming and thrash blasts of distortion power chords and delicate fingerstyle chord lead. When you see a symbol for a chord like C7sus4 do you close the music and back away slowly? What's the difference between a minor and a major? Just what is the scoop on chords? You've come to the right place to find out.

One of the finest features of the guitar is its ability to play almost any type of chord. You want a G7 augmented chord? Piece of cake on the guitar but don't try it on your saxophone. The versatility of the guitar as a chordal instrument brings with it the challenge of finding a way to understand its many possibilities. There are many different ways to play and categorize chords and many schemes for cataloguing them but this is a book about understanding the ways that chords are made, so that when you run into a new chord symbol you will be able to figure out how to play the chord in several different positions.

As we explore the properties of the fretboard, we will see how chords can be logically constructed from things that you probably already know. Your skill level as a guitarist is not a limiting factor in understanding the concept of chords. You will find that this approach to understanding chord forms applies not only to the first chords that you learned on the guitar, (probably an open G, C and D7) and is equally applicable to bar chords and more complex jazz chords.

It is important to understand that this is not a guitar technique book. It tells you the why and the where of chords but leaves the how and when entirely up to you. The purpose is to provide a step-by-step method of understanding guitar chord symbols and the musical sounds that they represent. This will enable *YOU* to play from sheet music, jazz charts and lead sheets, and the music collections known as fake books (just turn the page).

FAKE BOOKS, CHARTS, LEAD SHEETS
NOTATION, TABLATURE AND GRIDS

When you pick up a piece of sheet music, or a large collection of music that is known as a fake book, or even a the guitar part for a jazz big band arrangement you are often confronted with something that looks like the music below. Our goal is to find a way to translate these confusing chord symbols into shapes on the fretboard and sounds in our ears.

The music above is called a *lead sheet.* It has a melody and symbols for accompaniment chords. This format is common in fake books and music for recording studio sessions. Lead sheets give a great deal of information about a piece of music without specifying all of the parts but in order to really use them you must understand the chord symbols.

For the sake of clarity, the notes chords, intervals and scales in this book will be represented in three ways (four ways if you include imprecise and rambling prose). Standard notation, tablature, and fretboard grids will be shown for each example. The notation and tablature grids are staved together with each note having directly below it a *FRET* number on the string where that note should be played.

A picture of the fretboard is also attached. The shapes and patterns formed by the notes on the fretboard grid should be given particular attention. The physical relationships between notes and the effect this has on musical content is at the heart of understanding the concepts in this book. Below is a notation, tablature and grid representation of an open G major chord.

Important note: The numbers below the tablature refer to fret numbers. The circled numbers in the grid are suggested fingering only. Feel free to change any fingerings to suit your own technique.

G MAJOR

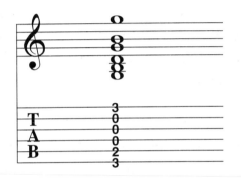

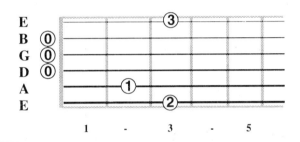

THE MYSTERIOUS FRETBOARD
FROM C TO SHINING C

Fretboard instruments like the guitar have some unique properties, not found on other instruments. The most important of these is the ability to play identical notes in different positions. For example; the C above middle C can only be played in one position on the piano.

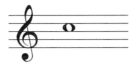

This is true of most instruments; one note and only one place to play that note. But lucky guitarists that we are, we get to chose from 5 musically identical C notes.

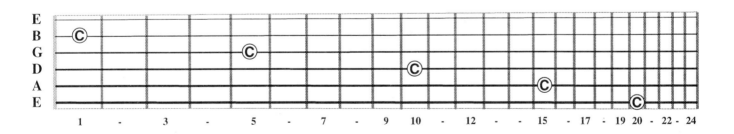

So, when it comes to reading music, guitarists are at a disadvantage because we are not only finding C but must also decide **WHICH C.**

PATTERNS PATTERNS EVERYWHERE

However, there is a plus side to this fretboard weirdness that is very valuable. Despite the fact that multiple positions for each note make sight reading a bit more difficult, the repeating patterns of the fretboard provide a very useful physical tool for understanding the musical properties of chords.

WHAT THE HECK DOES THAT MEAN?

Let's start with an example. The C on the 3rd fret of the A string and the C on the 5th fret of the G string are a set distance, known as an octave (8th) apart.

C Octave

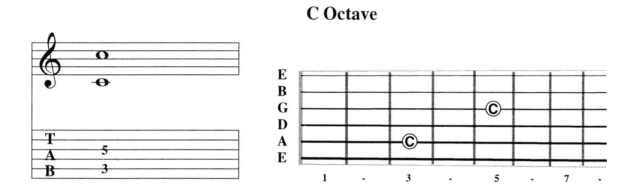

The physical shape shown on the fret board keeps the musical shape of an octave **REGARDLESS** of where it is placed on the A and G strings.

D Octave

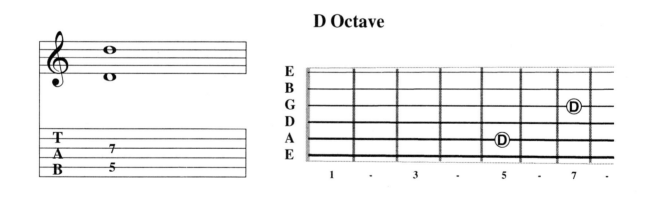

Moveable shapes
make the fretboard unique

This ability to move a physical shape up and down the fretboard without changing the musical relationship of the notes is a key concept. This concept of moveable shapes is the foundation of understanding and creating chords on the guitar.

A moveable shape can be the distance between 2 notes (known as an interval). The C and D octaves are examples of an interval.

It can be a pattern of from 3 to 6 notes that form a particular type of chord. The open G chord on page 4 is an example of this.

Finally, it can be a pattern specifying the notes used in any type of scale. There will be an example of this in the next chapter. The critical idea is that patterns and shapes can be moved up and down the fretboard and the musical relationship between the notes will *NOT CHANGE!*

CHANGE THE SHAPE-CHANGE THE SOUND

The other property of the fretboard that is essential to understanding chords is the way that physical changes of a shape on the fretboard affect the sound. Put another way, if the physical shape of a chord is changed, the musical shape will also be changed in a *LOGICAL* and *PREDICTABLE* way. For example, if we change the Octave (8th) in either the C or D octave by lowering the upper note of the octave by 2 frets, we have created an *interval* called either a minor 7th or a flatted 7th. This flatted 7th is also a moveable shape and remains a flatted 7th regardless of where we place it on the A and G strings. We will discover that this is a very commonly used interval in several types of chords. Turn the page for some flatted 7ths (♭7).

FLATTED 7TH INTERVAL

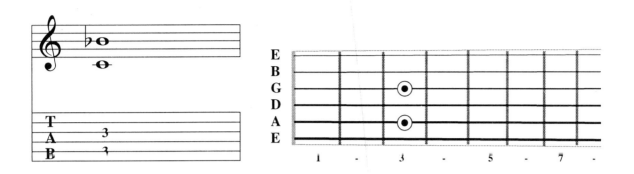

It is a moveable shape so, **MOVE IT!**

ANOTHER FLATTED 7TH INTERVAL

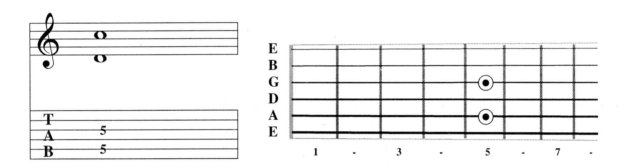

PLAYBREAK
Sevens & Eights

There are several different intervals in this exercise. We will use 3rds, 5ths, ♭7ths (flat 7ths) and 8ths (octaves) as some of the building blocks of chords.

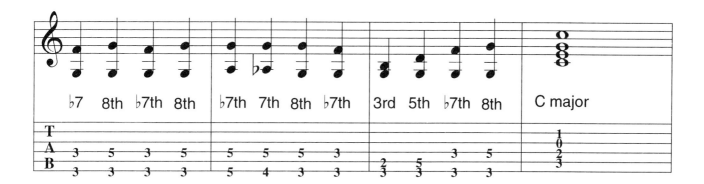

WHAT THIS BOOK IS GONNA DO FOR YOU

In order to gain a better understanding of what is up (and down) on the fretboard we will start with things that you already know how to play. In fact the chord concepts we will be using have their basis in only four simple open chord forms. By starting with four of the most common major chords (C, E, A, D) we can develop a system for understanding intervals within the chord and how the ***PHYSICAL and MUSICAL Shapes*** of chords are related to each other. Rather than memorizing chord shapes with no particular reference points, we will begin with major chord shapes that are familiar and examine what happens when we change notes or add notes to them.

Chapter One will introduce you to the concept of taking a chord that you already know and making something new from it. We will take an open C major chord and move the shape up and down the fretboard. Next we'll see what happens when we change one of the intervals of the chord.

Chapter Two will tell you the secrets of chord symbols and chord names. Every chord fits in a family and has certain common intervals with other family members. The charts in this chapter tell you exactly what intervals are needed to build all the chords you will ever need.

Chapter Three starts our exploration of chord shapes. In this chapter we move the shape of an open E chord around the fretboard. We will also change the intervals in the E major shape to make a number of new chord shapes and sounds.

Chapter Four will start with the open A major chord. This shape can also be moved around the neck and altered to make new chord shapes and sounds.

Chapter Five and Chapter Six will feature the open C major and open D major shapes. Each of these shapes will provide new ways to build chord shapes and sounds.

The final chapter will give a few interesting examples of things that you may have played or heard without understanding. It will also provide some practical tips and exercises for using the things that we have learned.

Throughout the book, there will be short musical examples called **_PLAYBREAKS_** that will let you test drive the new chords, get used to the new sounds and hear how these sounds fit together.

My experience in teaching guitar tells me that many players first learned to play by ear (as I did) and because of this we can be intimidated by chord names and symbols that are unfamiliar. When you come across an _UNKNOWN_ chord you will be able to combine knowledge that you already have with the rules and insights provided in this book to make sense of unknown chords by giving them logical form and shape.

With a little study and practice, chord symbols in fake book style collections, sheet music in any style, jazz lead sheets and big band charts will stop being scary and start being fun to play. Soon you will have the tools to create for yourself the shapes and the sounds that match the chord symbols.

CHAPTER ONE
The Tools for Understanding Guitar Chords

How many times have you opened up a piece of music and come face to face with a chord symbol that you had no clue of how to play? Play a C minor 7 flat5 or a F♯ 7 sus4 or whatever!! Many guitarists would take one look at the chord symbols below and head right back to Johny B. Goode.

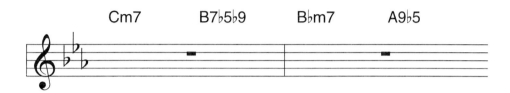

The main purpose of this book is to take the mystery and confusion out of chord symbols and names. We will do this by understanding the *MUSICAL* and *PHYSICAL* shapes of chords on the fretboard. How changes in the physical shape of a chord alters the sound and the chord's name and symbol. In order to understand chords, let's define the chord's component parts and understand a few simple rules.

Rule 1- Every chord is made up of 3 or more *DIFFERENT* notes

Rule 2- The note that gives a chord it's name is called the *ROOT*. For example, the root of a C minor 7 chord is C. In this book, the root is always the lowest note in a chord (well almost always).

Rule 3- The other notes in the chord are defined by their musical distance from the root note. This distance is called an *INTERVAL. A ROOT POSITION MAJOR* chord will always be our reference point. Every root position major chord contains the root (the lowest note), 3rd (the third note of the major scale), and 5th (the fifth note of the major scale).

Rule 4- By changing existing intervals to make new intervals, we can alter the *MUSICAL SHAPE* of the chord. In other words when we change the physical shape of the chord, we also change the chord name *AND* the sound of the chord.

Rule 5-The *PHYSICAL SHAPE* (where the fingers are placed) of a chord position is directly related to the *MUSICAL SHAPE* (chord name and sound). If the physical shape of a chord is not changed it can be moved up or down the fretboard without changing its musical shape.

Rule 6-The name of *any chord* specifies the notes in that chord. For example, if the chord name is C7 it will have a flatted 7th somewhere in it. By learning the meaning of a few terms like major and minor, you will gain a new understanding of chords.

Rule 7-Relax, have fun and make music. This is not as complicated as it sounds. Remember we will start with open position chords that you probably already know.

The fun begins on the next page.

THE CASE OF THE C MAJOR CHORD

Here is a **C major chord** represented in notation, tablature and fret grid. (The symbol for this chord is C, if the chord symbol is only the letter, it is a major chord).

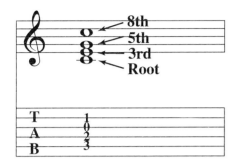

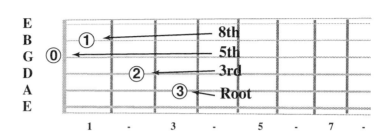

And a **C major scale** represented in notation, tablature, and fret grid

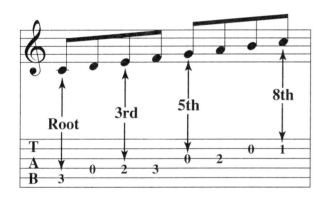

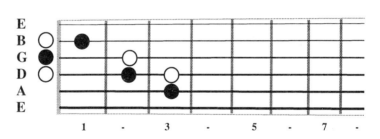

Let's compare the notes in the chord with the notes in the scale. Check it out. The C is the first note of the scale which we will always call the *root.* The E is third note of the scale (the *3rd)* the G is the fifth note of the scale (the *5th)* and the next note is C again, the eighth note of the scale, sometimes called an *octave* (8 notes in an octave-8 tentacles on an octopus-8 days a week). When we start to make new chords, we will call this the *8th.*

So now we know that *ANY* major chord consists of a Root (1), a 3rd, a 5th and maybe an 8th (octave). Here comes the coolest part. Let's take the physical *SHAPE* of the C chord and transfer that shape UP exactly two frets. Note that we are only transferring the 4 inside strings (A, D, G, B) and that the open string in the C chord is included in the new shape but must now be covered with a finger (the first finger).

D chord (major)

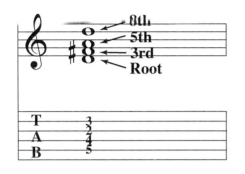

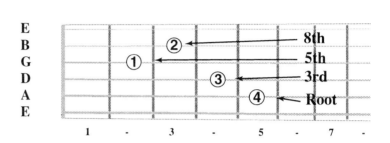

VOILA! a D MAJOR chord Note: the physical shape and the musical shape (major) remain the same. AND if we transfer the SHAPE of the C Major scale up two frets, we have a D MAJOR scale.

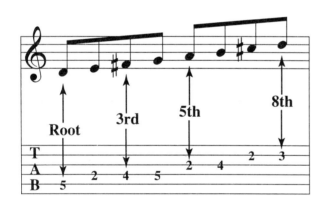

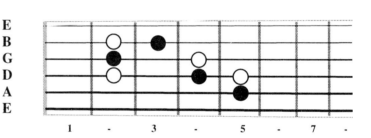

14

NEW RULE-The physical *SHAPES* of chords *AND* scales can be transferred anywhere on the fretboard (staying on the same strings) without changing their musical *SHAPES* (in our example, *MAJOR*)

MAKE NEW CHORDS BUT KEEP THE OLD ONES

Okay, we know what a C major shape looks like. But suppose you are looking at a piece of music that has a chord name that you don't know. Say for example the music has the symbol *Cmaj7*. This is the symbol for a C major 7 chord. From the name, you know that the root is C and that a *MAJOR* chord has a 3rd (E) and a 5th (G). Now look at the C major scale and add the 7th note (B) of the scale to the chord. The easiest way to find the 7th is to go to the note that is the octave or 8th. If we lower the 8th 1 fret it becomes a 7th. Thinking of the 7th in this way is really the key to understanding how the physical shape of a chord affects the musical shape. The process that we just went through to create a C major 7 shape will be repeated again and again to create other chord types so getting a good grasp of the concept is very important. Here is the shape of C maj7 in tablature, notation, and grid.

C major 7

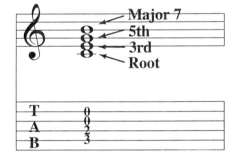
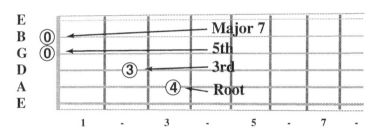

Play it! It has a very specific sound as well. I like to give every chord a personality. I used this one a lot on the Holiday Inn circuit so I think of it as the "Lounge Lizard". It is important not only to be able to understand chords but also to begin to recognize their sounds and musical contexts.

Now you know the shape of C maj7. You also know a D maj7 or F maj7 or any maj7. Just move the shape 2 frets up the fretboard.

D major7

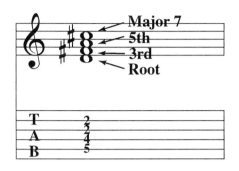
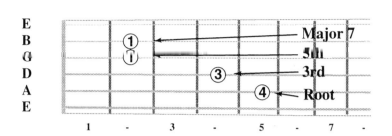

Onward to a Cmaj9. Again start with a major chord where C is the root, E the 3rd, and G the 5th. The key to this one is again the second C note or *8th.* If we move the *8th* up 2 frets, it becomes a *9th* Thus by raising the C (8) up 2 frets to D (9) we have added a 9th to a C major chord and created a

Cmaj9 chord

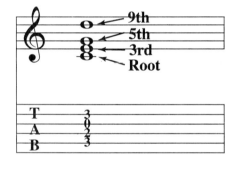
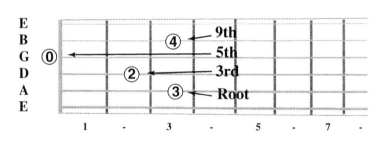

This major 9 shape can also be moved up the neck to any fret position.

Try a D major9

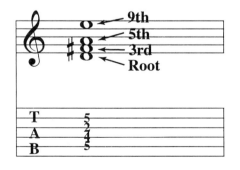
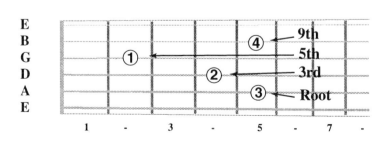

PLAYBREAK
C's the Day

This first playbreak takes two open chords and changes their respective sounds by changing only one note at the time. We've already talked about the three C chords. Use your new insights to see how we named the three A chords. Listen closely to the sound of each chord. Understanding a chord is only useful if you can hear the beauty of it's sound. You can strum this progression or try out some finger picking. Experiment with the chords and most of all **listen!**

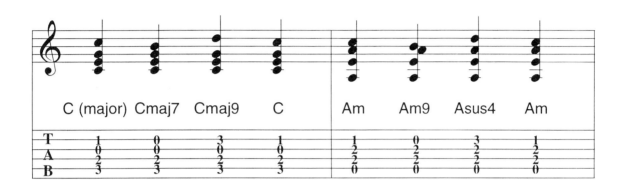

SUMMARY

So to summarize the ideas in this chapter. The open C major chord is made up of a root, 3rd, 5th and 8th. If we preserve the *PHYSICAL* shape of the chord, it can be moved up the neck without changing the *MUSICAL* shape (major). Remember, wherever we put the chord gives the chord it's note name. So if the root note is on F♯ then it becomes an F♯ major chord.

The major form can be changed by raising or lowering the *INTERVALS* that make up the chord. Intervals are the musical distance of notes in the chord from the *ROOT* note. We created a C major 7 chord by lowering the 8th (octave) to the 7th note of the C major scale and we created a C major 9 by raising the 8th to the 9th note of the C major scale *AND* because of the magical way shapes can be move up the neck without changing their *MUSICAL SHAPE,* we now know a shipload of major7 and major 9 chords.

At this point if you are unsure of these ideas it would be a good time to review Chapter 1. On the other hand, if this stuff is too easy for you, I still have plenty of time to confuse you. Try the exercises for Chapter One, they will give a better understanding of how to move shapes around the neck. After you write out a chord, always work on playing it and always *LISTEN* carefully to the sound.

EXERCISES
for
CHAPTER ONE

1.) In tablature and fretboard grid, write an F major 7th chord (notation is extra credit)

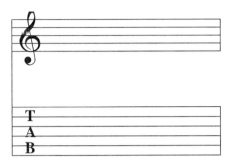
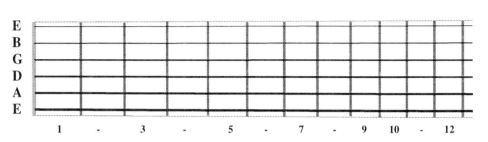

2.) In tablature and fretboard grid, write an A major 9th chord (notation too if you're brave)

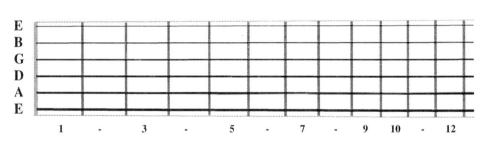

3.)   Find and play the following chords - G major - F major 7th - B flat major - E flat major 7th - F major 9th (remember, we're starting with the basic *SHAPE* of an open C chord for all of these.)

CHAPTER TWO
WHAT'S IN A NAME

Look at the chord symbols below. The first one is 'G' . But its full name is G *major.* The second is C *minor.* The next is F *seventh.* But its full name is F *dominant seventh.* The last is B flat *diminished seventh.*

Understanding the *symbols* and the *names* is the first step in understanding the chords.

IT'S ALL IN THE FAMILY

The four chord symbols above are examples of the 4 different chord families. These families are *Major, Minor, Dominant and Altered.* All chords fall into one of these families and have common characteristics with other chords in the same family.

In order to understand how chords really work, we need to be able to look at a chord symbol and put that chord in it's correct family. Each family has specific intervals that give the family its characteristic sound. By classifying the chord as major, minor, dominant or altered we will have already specified some of the notes and intervals in the chord.

Major family chord symbols can be as simple as a letter name. For example the symbol *A* means A *Major.* Other major chords contain the symbol *maj* as in *A maj7* (A major 7th) or *A maj9* (A major 9th). The exception to this is the symbol for a 6th chord. *A6* means *A major* 6th.

Minor family chord symbols always state their minor status with either a lower case *"m"* or the "-" sign. So *Am or A-* both mean A minor. *F#m9* or *F#-9* both mean F sharp minor 9th.

Dominant family chord symbols are always a note name directly followed by either a *"7"*, *"9"* or *"13"*. So, D7 means D dominant 7th , D9 means D dominant 9th and D13 means D dominant 13th. Dominant chords **never** have *m* or - in the name.

Altered chords? At this point let's just say that anything not major, minor, or dominant is altered. Altered symbols include diminished (o), half diminished (ø), suspended 4th (sus4), and 7th suspended 4th (7sus4). We'll consider each altered chord individually.

FAMILY AFFAIR
THE INTERVALS THAT MAKE UP EACH CHORD FAMILY

MAJOR CHORDS are very important to us. We will create every other chord by changing the shape of a *major* chord. We will use four different major shapes to build all other chords. All four of these shapes contain the same note intervals. These intervals are *root, 3rd, 5th and 8th (octave)*.

C major

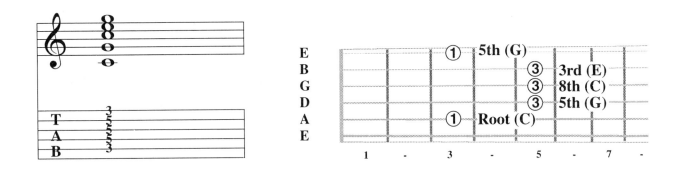

MINOR CHORDS can be made from any *major chord* by locating the *3rd* lowering it one fret. Minor chords contain the following intervals: Root, *flat 3rd (lowered one fret)* 5th and octave or 8th.

C minor

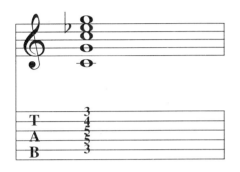

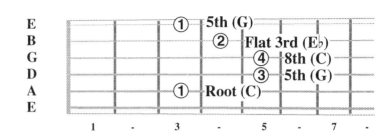

DOMINANT CHORDS can be made from any *major chord* by finding the *8th (octave)* and lowering it 2 frets. This creates *a flat 7th interval.* Dominant chords contain a *root, 3rd (not a flat 3rd), 5th, and always have a FLAT 7TH.*

C dominant 7

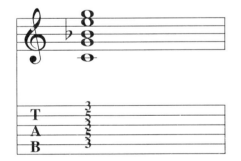

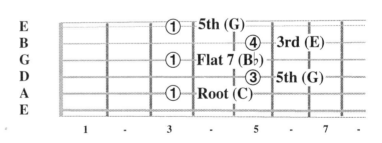

21

ALTERED CHORDS are chords that do not fit in any other category. In this book, we will consider only the following altered chords: suspended 4ths (sus4), seventh suspended 4ths (7sus4), diminished (o), and half diminished (ø). (Students of music theory, please be gentle with me. The categories and terminology that I have devised for this chord book are very useful in understanding chord shapes on the guitar but may not always match traditional music theory.)

There is one more category that needs to be discussed to provide you with all the necessary tools to read sheet music and charts. We will call these the **SLASH CHORDS.**

SLASH CHORDS have nothing to do with Guns n Roses. Examples are C/G and Dm/C. C/G means C major with a G note as the bass (lowest) note and Dm/C means D minor with C as the bass (lowest) note. Slash chords are sometimes called inversions. We will talk more about this in later chapters.

The charts on the next pages give the *chord name and chord symbol(s)* for a variety of chords. The *intervals* that make up each chord are also listed. By always starting with a major chord it is easy to compare the intervals in other chords, change them to match the listed intervals and construct any other chord type.

HERE ARE SOME OF THE CHORDS YOU WILL WANT TO KNOW

symbol	name	family	required intervals	optional intervals

MAJOR FAMILY

symbol	name	family	required intervals	optional intervals
C	C major	major	root, 3rd, 5th	8th (octave)
C6	C major 6	major	root, 3rd, 5th, 6th	8th
C maj7	C major 7	major	root, 3rd, 5th, 7th	
C maj9	C major 9	major	root, 3rd, 9th	5th

MINOR FAMILY

symbol	name	family	required intervals	optional intervals
Cm	C minor	minor	root, flat 3rd, 5th	8th
Cm6	C minor 6	minor	root, flat 3rd, 6th	8th
Cm7	C minor 7	minor	root, flat 3rd, 5th, flat 7	8th
Cm9	C minor 9	minor	root, flat 3rd, flat 7, 9th	5th, 8th

DOMINANT FAMILY

symbol	name	family	required intervals	optional intervals
C7	C dominant 7	dominant	root, 3rd, flat 7	5th, 8th
C9	C dominant 9	dominant	root, 3rd, flat 7, 9th	5th
C7♭9	C dom.7 flat 9	dominant	root, 3rd, flat 7, flat 9	
C7♯9	C dom.7 sharp 9	dominant	root, 3rd, flat 7, sharp9	
C7♯5 or C7+	C dom.7 sharp 5 or C dom.7 augmented	dominant	root, 3rd, flat 7, sharp5	
C13	C thirteen	dominant	root, 3rd, flat 7, 6th	8th

ALTERED FAMILY

symbol	name	family	required intervals	optional intervals
Co7	C diminished 7	altered	root, flat 3rd, flat 5, 6	
Csus4	C suspended 4th	altered	root, 4th, 5th	8th
C7sus4	C 7 suspended 4th	altered	root, 4th, 5th, flat7th	8th
Cm7♭5 or C∅	Cminor7 flat 5 or C half diminished*	altered	root, flat 3rd, flat 5th, flat 7	

*C Minor 7 flat 5 and C half diminished are two names for the same chord, either symbol is correct.

23

CHART OF CHORD FAMILIES, CHORD TYPES AND INTERVALS

Chord Type Intervals

Chord Type	Root	Flat 3rd	Maj 3rd	4th	Flat 5th	5th	#5th	6th	Flat 7th	Maj 7th	Octave (8th)	Flat9	Maj9	#9th
MAJOR														
Major	x		x			x					(x)			
Maj7	x		x			(x)				x	(x)			
Maj6	x		x			(x)		x			(x)			
Maj9	x		x			(x)				x	(x)		x	
MINOR														
Minor	x	x				x								
Min6	x	x				(x)		x			(x)			
Min7	x	x				(x)			x		(x)			
Min9	x	x				(x)			x		(x)		x	
DOMINANT														
Dom7	x		x			(x)			xx					
Dom9	x		x			(x)			xx		(x)		x	
Dom7b9	x		x			(x)			xx		(x)	x		
Dom7#9	x		x			(x)			xx					x
Dom7b5	x		x		xxx				xx		(x)			
Dom7#5	x		x				xxx		xx		(x)			
13th	x		x			(x)		x	xx					
ALTERED														
Diminished	x	x			x			x						
Sus4	x			xxx		x					(x)			
Min7b5	x	x			xxx				x					
7sus4	x			xxx		(x)			xx		(x)			

KEY: X means the chord **MUST** contain the interval
(X) means the chord **MAY** contain the interval
XXX means the interval is specified in the chord **NAME**
XX emphasizes that all dominant chords **MUST** have a flat 7th

HOW TO USE THE CHARTS

The charts in this chapter provide a lot of information without giving you a clue on how to apply it. ***Don't panic!*** The hardest part is over. In order to start creating chords on your own, you just need to follow a few simple steps and rules.

RULE 1 - *Always begin with a major chord shape*

If you are reading through music and you find the symbol *Dm7b5* which translates to the chord name D minor 7 flat 5. You start with a D major chord and label the intervals. (D shapes are in chapter 5.)

RULE 2 - *Compare the intervals of the new chord with the major chord that has the same root note.*

In our *Dm7b5,* the ***m*** tells us that the 3rd is lowered one fret to a *b**3rd (flat 3rd),*** the 5th is lowered one fret to a *b**5th (flat 5th),*** and as there is no 7th in the major chord we need to lower the 8th by 2 frets to a *b**7th (flat 7th).***

RULE 3 - *Take the major shape and change it to match the new intervals (just like on the next page).*

Our target chord is a **Dm 7♭5** so let's start with a garden variety open D major chord. Now label the intervals in the major chord.

D Major

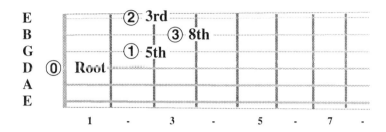

Now take our D major chord, *to make it minor we lower the 3rd by one fret , lower the 5th by one fret to make a flatted 5th* and since we don't have a 7th, we'll make one *by lowering our 8th by two frets* to a flatted *7th* and *presto—*

Dm7♭5 (half diminished)

This method of changing *major chord shapes that we know into new chord shapes* is a useful method of expanding our chord vocabulary. At the same time, it increases our understanding of chords.

The rest of this book will start with the familiar open major chord shapes: E, A, C, and D. By changing notes within these shapes, and moving the results around the fretboard, we will be able to play a great variety of chords in a number of positions. We will always make a new chord from a major shape that we already know and understand.

PLAYBREAK
MESSIN' WITH THE 'D'

In this chord progression, we will start with a D major and change the *8th* interval to get a ***D major 7th (Dmaj7) and a D major 6th (D6).*** In the second measure, we raise and lower the 3rd to get ***D suspended 4th and a D suspended 2nd.*** In the last two measures, the same chords are played as arpeggios.

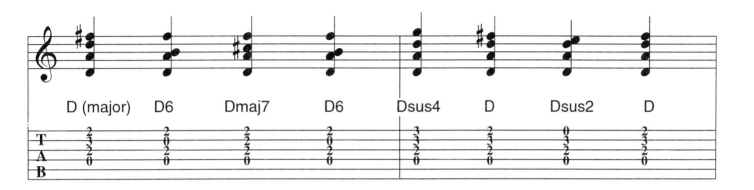

CHAPTER 2 EXERCISES

1. Write the symbol for the following chords

    a) G major   _____
    b) D minor   _____
    c) A Dominant ninth _____
    d) E♭ minor seventh _____
    e) G♯ diminished   _____
    f) F major seventh _____

2. Write the name of the following chord symbols

    a) D-   _____
    b) Cmaj9   _____
    c) F   _____
    d) Am7♭5   _____
    e) C7sus4   _____
    f) D9   _____
    g) Gm7   _____

3. What intervals are in the following chord families

    a) Major   _____
    b) Minor   _____
    c) Dominant _____

4. What intervals are in the following chord types

    a) maj7   _____
    b) m   _____
    c) 9   _____
    d) m9   _____
    e) sus4   _____
    f) 7♭9   _____

CHAPTER THREE

HOW TO CREATE CHORDS
FROM THE "E" MAJOR SHAPE

The shape below is E major. It is represented in notes, tab and grid form.

E chord

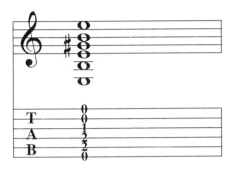 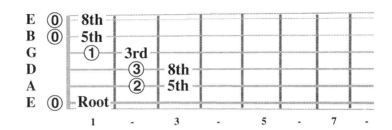

We know from the introductory chapter that this shape can be moved anywhere on the fretboard and still be a **major chord.** Since moving this chord shape requires you to place the index finger (1) all the way across the fretboard and the shape comes from an E chord , these chords are called **E form Bar chords.** Moving the shape to the 3rd fret makes it a G major. Remember, this is the shape we will use to create new chords. The most important thing to remember is the position of the **3rds, 5ths, and 8ths** within the chord shape . All of our new chord shapes will be made by manipulating the intervals of major chord shapes.

G bar chord

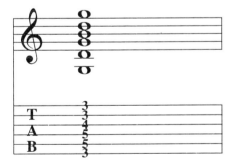 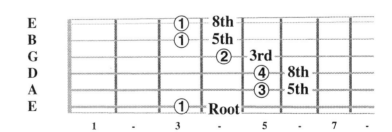

How about a G major 7th (Gmaj7). We only need to change one note of our major chord to create a major 7th. Take the 8th (octave) on the D string and lower it by 1 fret. Now we have a moveable **major 7th (maj7) chord** (note: the G on the high E string should be played lightly or not at all)

Gmaj7

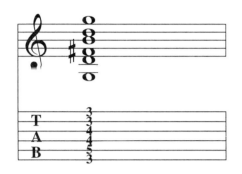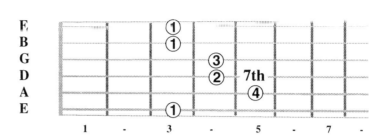

How about a **Minor chord?** We only need to make one change in our major chord. If we flat *the 3rd* (lower it by one fret) we get a moveable minor (m). In this case Gm.

Gm or G-

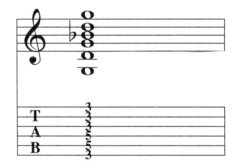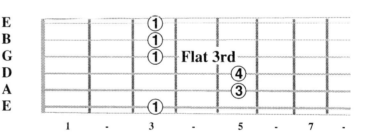

Let's keep it in the family and make a **Minor 7th (m 7 or -7).** Start with the major, lower the 3rd, *then lower the 8th two frets on the D string to a flat 7.* Here we have a moveable minor 7th (m7).

Gm7(G-7)

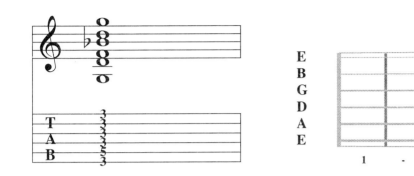

Remember the *Dominant* family of chords? In chapter 2 we learned that they have a root, 3rd, and *a flat 7th.* To make a Dominant 7th from our Major, we only need to Lower the 8th on the D string by 2 frets. Remember, to make a *major 7th* we lowered the *8th by one fret to a 7th—here* we lower the *8th two frets to a flatted 7th* to make a *Dominant 7th.*

G7

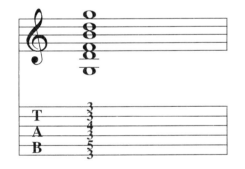
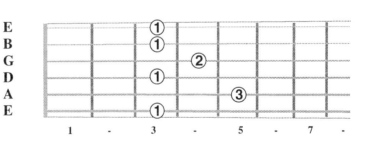

Here is our first Altered chord. From the charts in Chapter 2, we know that a suspended 4th chord has a root, 4th, 5th and 8th. From our major chord, we only need to raise the 3rd by one fret.

Gsus4

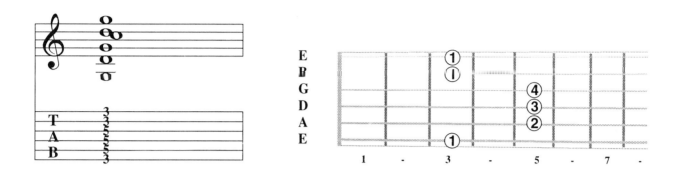

And for the 7th suspended 4th just lower the 8th by two frets to a flat 7th.

G7sus4

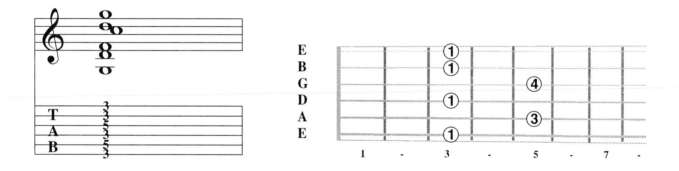

The best part is that **all of the above chords are MOVEABLE to ANYWHERE on the fretboard.**

PLAYBREAK
Turn Your Blues Around

We'll put our new chords to work in a progression that could be used at the end of a Chicago style blues like *Stormy Monday.* Listen to the smooth chromatic (one fret at a time) downward movement of the chords finally coming to rest (resolving in theory talk) on G major 7th. (This is also an example of a chord substitution but more on that later. For now play, listen and add these sounds to your vocabulary.)

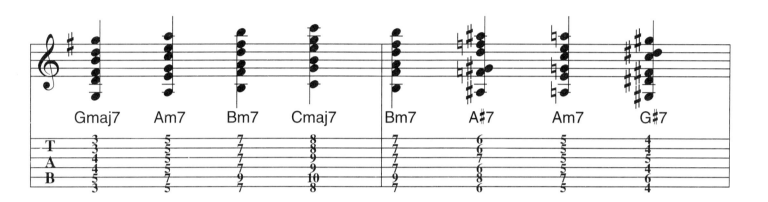

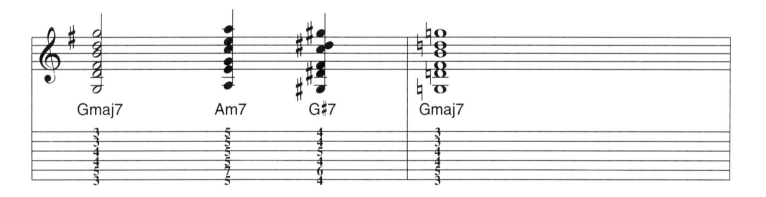

SELECTING NOTES FROM E FORM BAR CHORDS

By now you have a good understanding of how to make *E form bar chords.* Let's try something a bit more interesting. Instead of using the index finger to bar across all the strings, let's choose only the notes we need to play the desired chord. As you can see below, there are duplicate notes in the bar form (5ths on A and B strings and 8ths on D and high E strings).

G bar shape

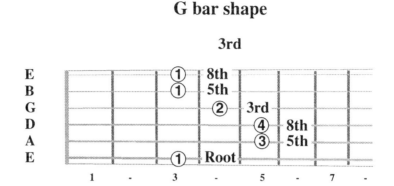

Lets remove the 5th on the A string, and the 8th on the High E string. Because we are skipping the *A and E strings,* these chords are formed on broken sets of strings. They are referred to as *broken string shapes.*

G broken shape

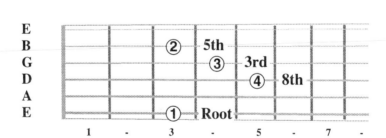

By changing these four notes in various way, we can create a great many interesting chord shapes. These broken shapes are easier to play than bar chords. They also have a less cluttered sound since they eliminate doubled 5ths and octaves. You may have seen them before referred to as Modern Orchestral chords in other Mel Bay publications.

BROKEN CHORD SHAPES ON THE LOW E, D, G AND B STRINGS

Major Family Chords

To make a broken major 7th chord, lower the 8th on the D string by one fret to a 7th.

Gmaj7

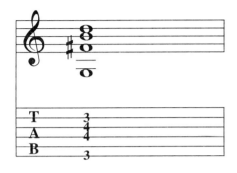 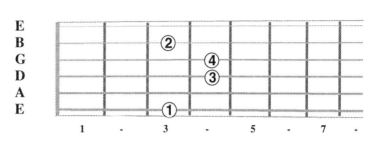

To make a broken Major 6th chord, lower the 8th on the D string three frets to a 6th.

G6

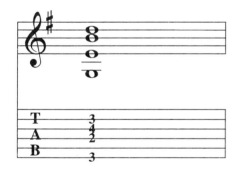 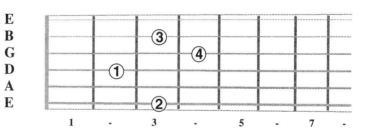

PLAYBREAK
Major Changes

    In Jazz Charts there are often long stretches when the guitar plays a major chord on each quarter note. To add variety it is okay to switch between a major 6th and a major 7th as shown below. In most cases, major family chords can be substituted for each other to add movement where there is only one chord written in the lead sheet or chart. This example is in the key of B♭ for a reason. Many Big Band charts are written by and for sax and trumpet players. These silly horn players have what are called B♭ instruments-that is what they call a C is actually a B♭-therefore they write in B♭ to make the charts easier for the horns (and consequently harder for a real instrument like guitar). If you want to play the more traditional types of jazz, get used to playing in F, B♭, Eb, and A♭. If a sax player gives you a hard time, have him play in E, F♯ or B major. You'll make your point.

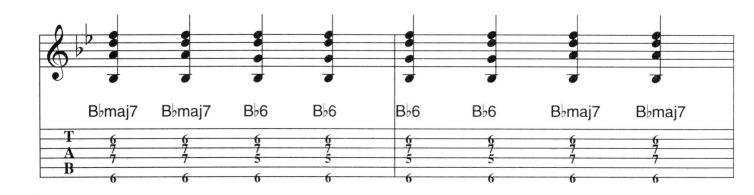

Dominant Chords
(Remember, all dominant chords have a major 3rd and a flat 7)

There are a number of broken shape dominant chords that are very useful because dominant chords can be substituted for each other in many playing situations.

To make a broken dominant 7th chord, lower the 8th on the D string by two frets to a flat seventh.

G7

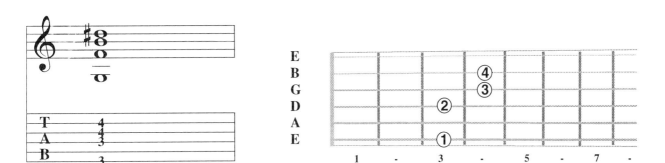

To make a 7th augmented, lower the 8th two frets to a flat 7 and raise the 5th on the B string one fret to a sharp 5th.

G7♯5 or G7+

37

To make a 7th flat 5th chord, lower the 8th by two frets and lower the 5th by one fret to a flat 5th. (Played by itself, this is a very odd sound but used in the right place, like the next Playbreak, it sounds great.)

G7♭5

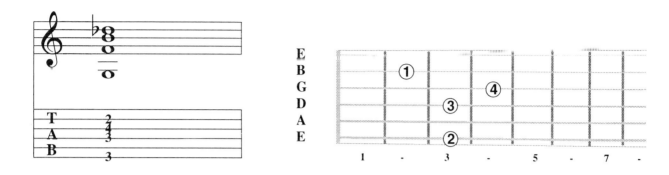

Here is an interesting one: To make a 13th, lower the 8th by two frets and raise the 5th on the B string two frets to a 6th. The name 13th comes from counting from the root past the 8th on to 13.

G13

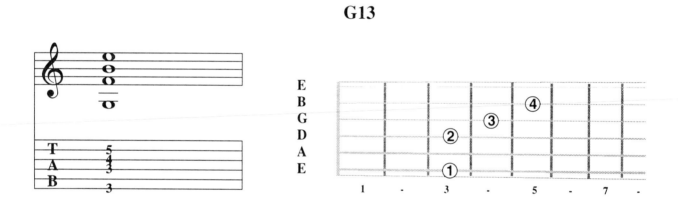

Minor Chords
(Remember: all minor chord have a flat 3rd)

To make a broken minor 7th, lower the 3rd on the G string one fret to a flat 3rd (minor 3rd) and lower the 8th on the D string by two frets to a flat 7th.

Gm7

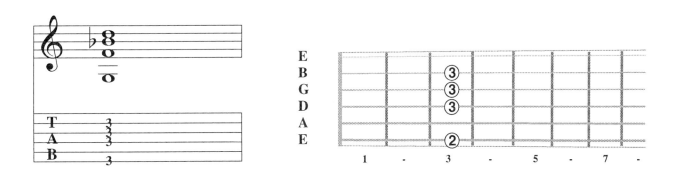

To make a minor 6th lower the 3rd by one fret and lower the 8th by 3 frets to a 6th.

Gm6

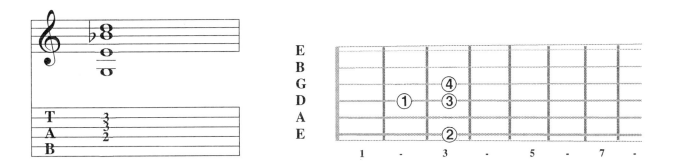

How about a minor 11th chord? Lower the 3rd to make a minor. Now, like our 13th, count through the octave to find the 11th. The 11th is also a 4th so we could call this chord a minor 7th suspended 4th. We add the 4th by lowering our 5th by 2 frets.

Gm7sus4 or Gm11

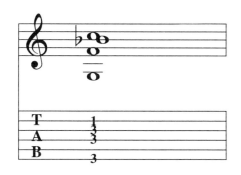
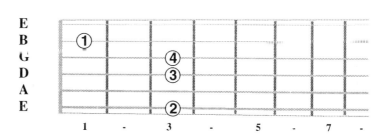

To make a minor with a major 7th (m/maj7) lower the 3rd and lower the 8th by one fret to a 7th.

Gm/maj7

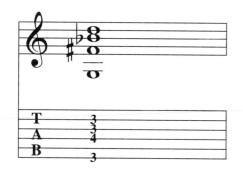
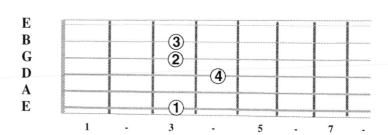

Altered Chords

To make a minor 7th flat 5 chord (also called a half diminished), lower the 3rd one fret for minor, lower the 5th one fret for a flat 5th, and lower the 8th two frets to a flat 7th.

Gm7♭5 or GØ

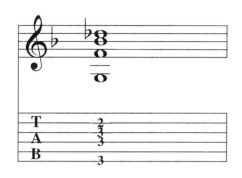
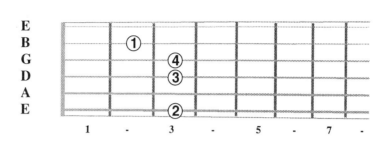

To make a full diminished chord, lower the 3rd, the 5th, and lower the 8th three frets to a double flat 7th. (The same note as a 6th.)

G⁰

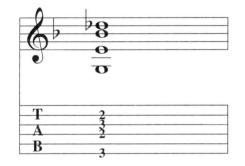
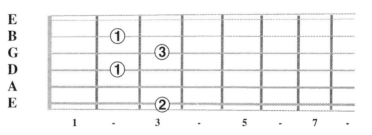

PLAYBREAK
THE WATERFALL

This series of broken chords will smoothly take you through several different keys before ending on F♯ major 7th. Listen to the movement of the individual voices as you play it and concentrate on having each finger move independently.

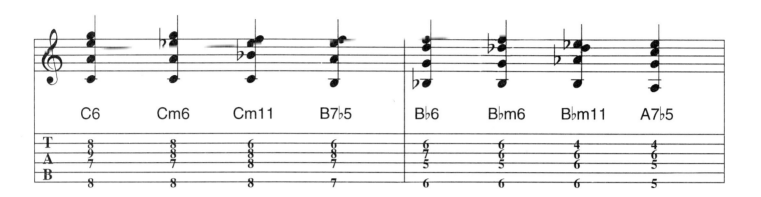

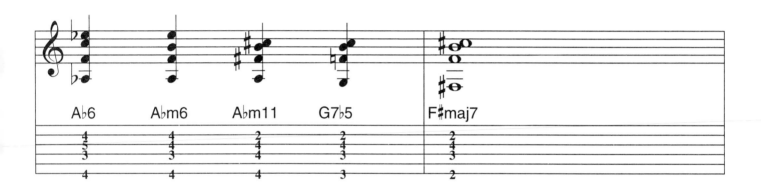

You can Waterfall starting and ending anywhere on the E string.

EXERCISE
LEARN THE NOTE NAMES

To make the best use of your new chords, learn the note name of each fret on the E string by filling in the missing notes. An easy way to find notes is by memorizing a few landmark frets and counting up and down to find the unknown notes. Each of the grids below have some landmarks on them—fill in the unmarked frets.

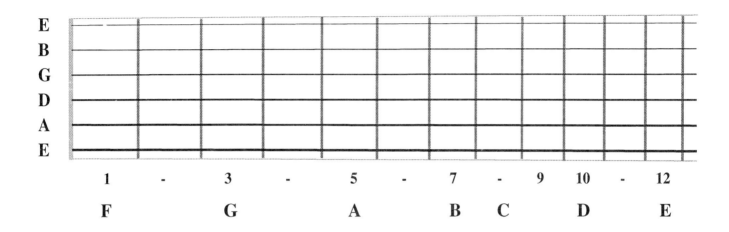

| 1 | - | 3 | - | 5 | - | 7 | - | 9 | 10 | - | 12 |
| F | | G | | A | | B | C | | D | | E |

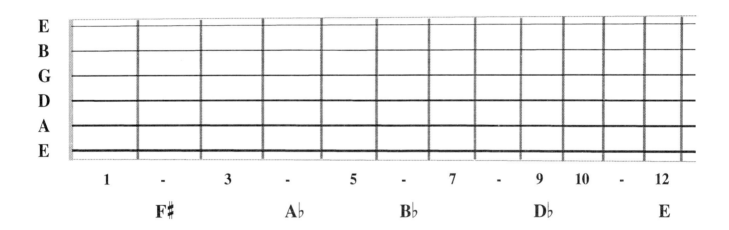

| 1 | - | 3 | - | 5 | - | 7 | - | 9 | 10 | - | 12 |
| | F♯ | | A♭ | | B♭ | | | D♭ | | | E |

EXERCISE
FIND THE CHORDS

1.) Play the following E form bar chords: F - Fmaj7 - A♭m7 - B♭sus4 - C7 - E♭m - B - Bmaj7 - Bm7 - Bsus4

2.) Play the following E form broken chords: F#6 - F#m7 - Gm11 - A♭7♭5 - B13   C7#5 - Am6 - Dm7♭5

3.) Play the following chords using either E form bar or broken shapes: A flat major 7 - B7♭5 - Cm7 - G7+5 - Aø - D♭ minor 6 - Do - D - E diminished - Al3 - F# half diminished

CHAPTER FOUR

HOW TO CREATE CHORDS
FROM THE "A" MAJOR SHAPE

Here we go again, same concept, different shape. This time the root note of the chord will be the A string.

The shape below is the A major open chord form.

A major chord

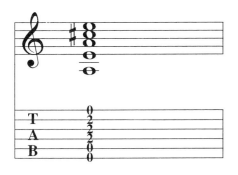 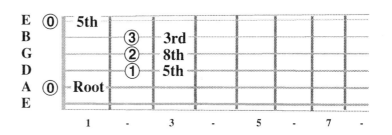

We know the this shape can be moved anywhere and remain a major chord. If we put this shape on the 3rd fret it becomes a C major.

C major chord

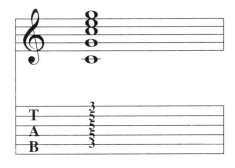 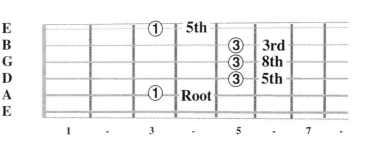

Let's stay in the major family and make a C major 7th chord by lowering the 8th to a 7th.

Cmaj7

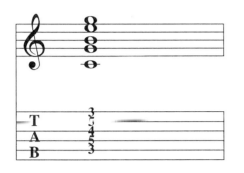 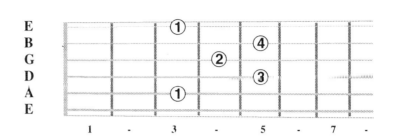

PLAYBREAK
Coal Train Turning

This progression puts together the major 7th shapes from the E and A strings. It is a typical John Coltrane style chord sequence and is used at the end of a progression to return to the begining. Chords used this way are called a *turnaround*.

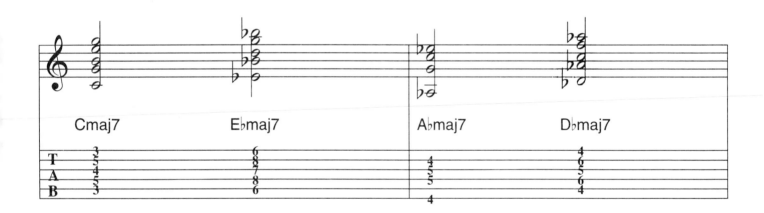

Cmaj7   Ebmaj7   Abmaj7   Dbmaj7

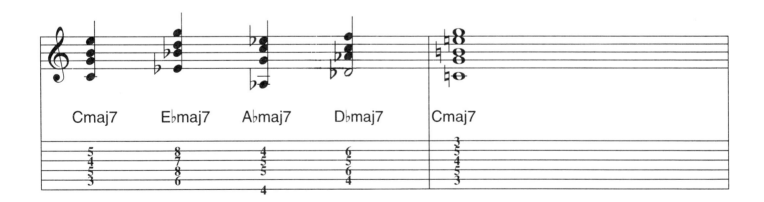

Cmaj7   Ebmaj7   Abmaj7   Dbmaj7   Cmaj7

How about a major 6th chord? Take the 5th on the E string and raise it 2 frets to a 6th. This chord is not one of my favorite voicings but it does have a sort of old fashioned charm.

C6

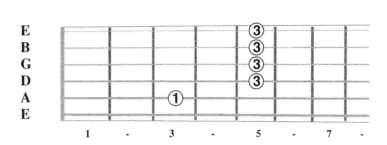

How about the minor family? Here is what it looks like when you lower the 3rd to make a minor chord.

Cm

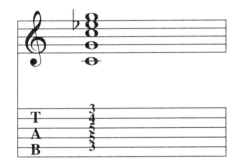

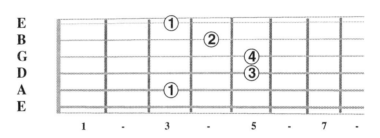

Keep it in the minor family with a flat 3rd, then lower the 8th on the G string to a flat 7th. This gives us a minor 7th chord.

Cm7

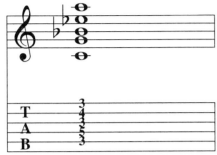
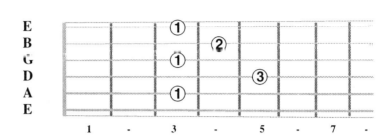

Remember our minor with a major 7th (m/maj7) in the E form? A lowered 3rd makes it minor and the 8th is lowered one fret for the major 7th. This is a chord that doesn't do well on it's own and is usually only used in passing as you will see in the next Playbreak.

Cm/maj7

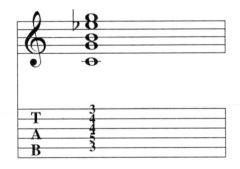
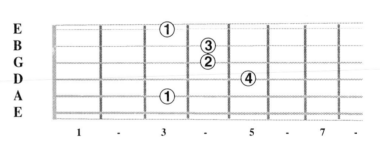

PLAYBREAK
Listen to Your Inner Voice

In this chord series, we will move the 8th of our A minor shape down and then back up one fret at a time. This is a very pleasing way to get some tension and motion into a passage where a minor chord is being held.

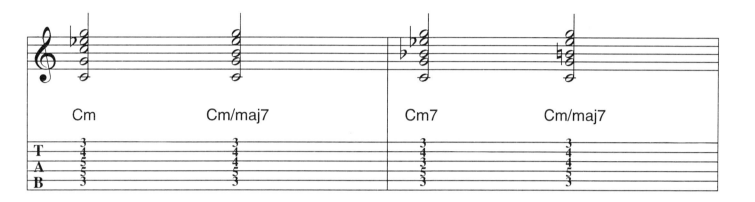

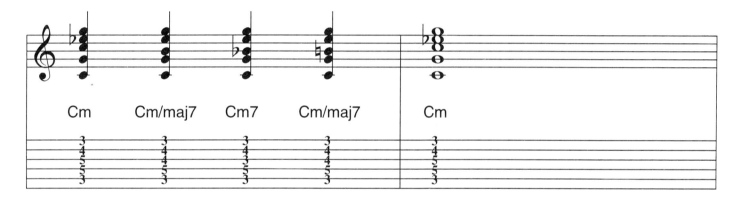

Time for a dominant 7th chord. The only change from the major is lowering the 8th on the G string by 2 frets to a flat 7th.

C7

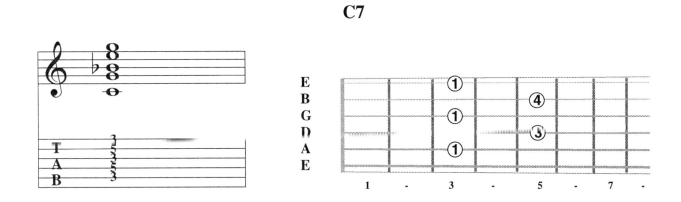

Now let's make a suspended 4th. Just raise the 3rd on the B string up one fret to a 4th.

Csus4

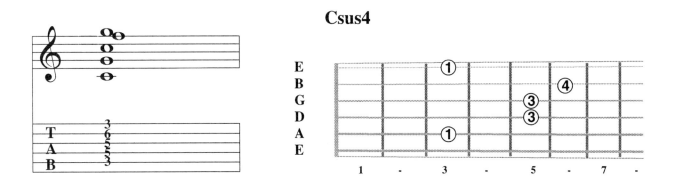

To get a 7th suspended 4th, raise the 3rd by one fret to a 4th, then lower the 8th by two frets to a flat 7th.

C7sus4

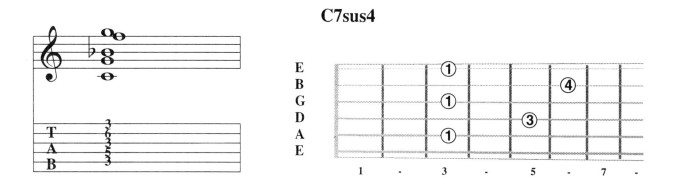

Partial "A" form chords

For the next two shapes, we will use only the inside four strings, the A,D,G and B strings. First, for a minor 7th flat 5th chord (half diminished) we lower the 3rd one fret to make it minor, then lower the 8th two frets to make it a flat 7th, finally, lower the 5th one fret to make a flat 5th.

Cm7♭5(C∅)

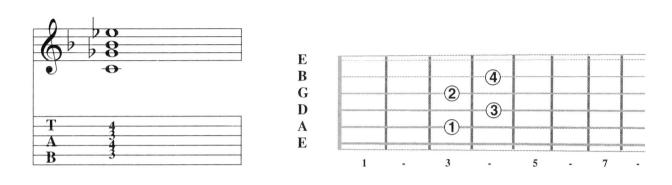

Now lets make a diminished chord. A diminished chord needs a flat 3rd, a flat 5th and a double flat 7th. So lower the 3rd one fret, lower the 5th one fret, and lower the 8th three frets.

C°

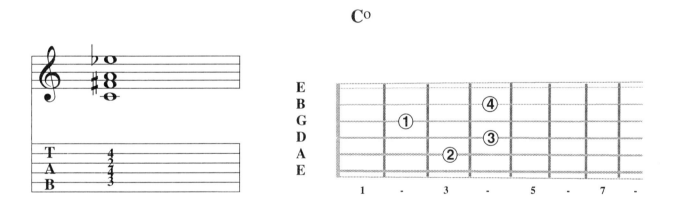

All of the shapes above are of course transferable to any fret position. By learning the E forms and the A forms, you can now play many chords in two different positions. This is very handy when reading chord charts since you will find that you will not need to move up and down the neck as far to find chords.

51

PLAYBREAK
Hold That Note

This chord sequence uses E and A shapes. We'll keep the highest note constant throughout and use descending chords and a descending bass note.

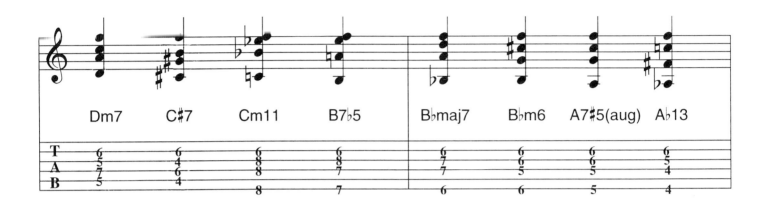

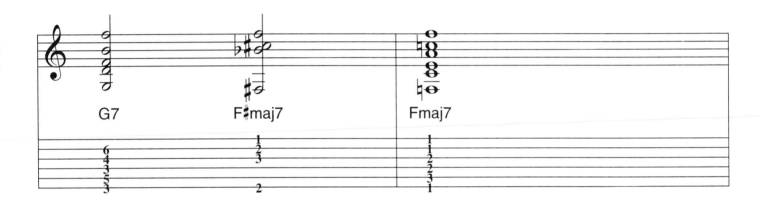

Measure 3 contains two E shapes that were not in Chapter 3. Look at the notes in these new chords and name the interval of each note.

EXERCISES

We now have a *GIANT* vocabulary of E and A form chords *BUT* in order to really use them we gotta learn our way a round the "hood". Since these chords all get their names from their root notes, we need to memorize the first 12 frets of the E and A strings.

Exercise 1—fill in the note names under each fret of the E string:

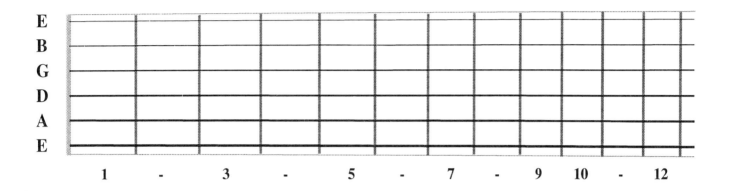

Exercise 2—fill in the note names on each fret of the A string:

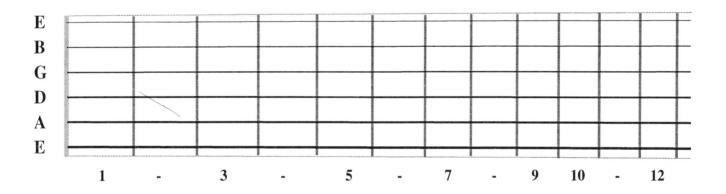

CHAPTER FIVE

MAKING CHORDS
FROM THE "C" CHORD FORM

What comes around goes around. We're back to the open C major chord from Chapter One. The C shape chords that we are going to look at in this chapter are quite different from E and A based chords. The order of intervals in both the E and A chords is: root-5th-8th-3rd while the order for the C is root-3rd-5th-8th. This different order gives us some neat new possibilities. As always we'll start with the major chord.

C

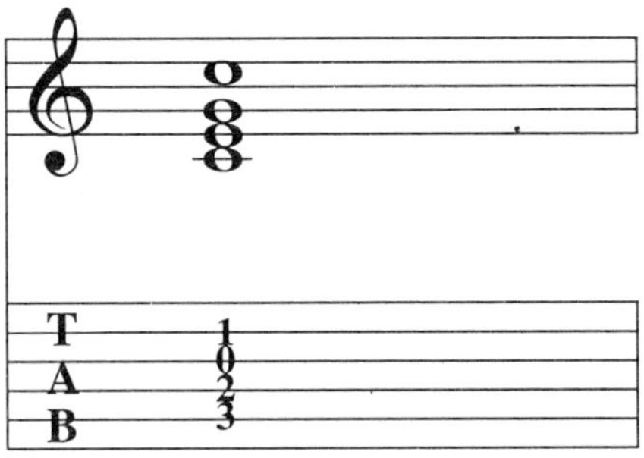

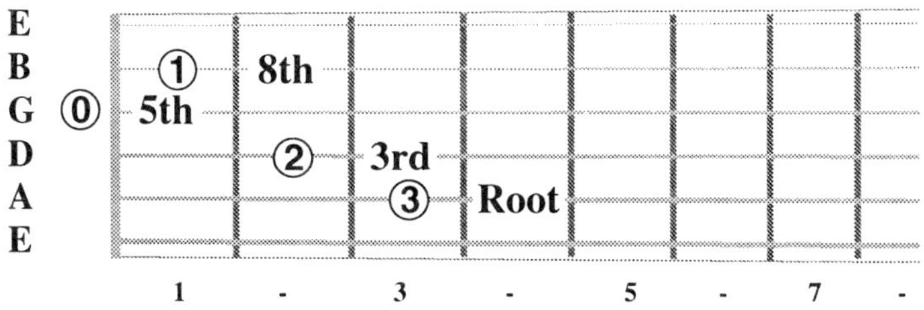

And we've seen that this major shape is moveable and remains a major chord wherever it is placed on the fretboard.

D

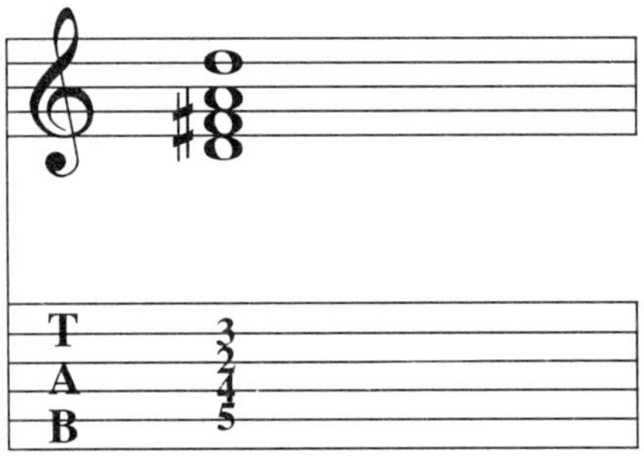

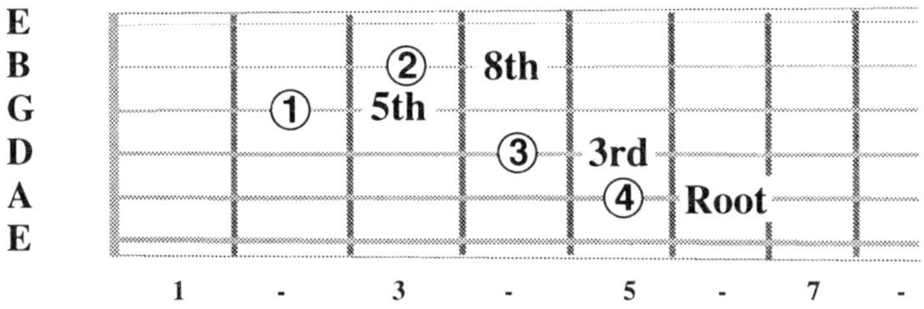

Because the sequence of notes (root, 3rd, 5th, 8th) in the C form differs from the sequence of notes in the A and E forms (root, 5th, 8th, 3rd, 5th), the possibilities for changing C chord forms are quite different. We can drop the 8th to a 7th for a Major 7th chord as we did in Chapter One.

Dmaj7

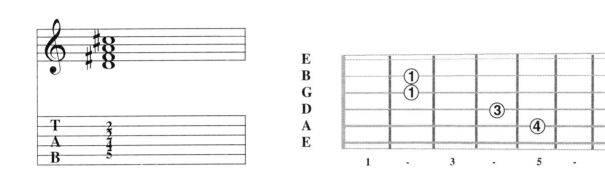

Remember when we raised the 8th two frets to a 9th for a major 9th chord in the first chapter?

Dmaj9

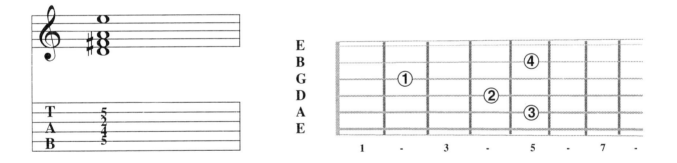

55

To stay in the major family, raise the 5th one fret to a 6th and we have a major 6th chord. This is a better sounding 6th chord than the A form 6th from the previous chapter (remember the root note is still on the A string.)

Dmaj6

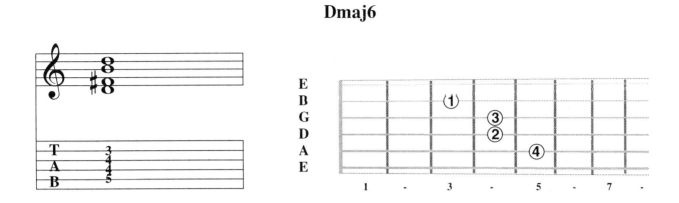

The C form works very well for making chords in the dominant family but our method of finding the flatted 7th is different. Instead of lowering the 8th as we did with the E and A shapes we'll raise the 5th three frets to get the flat 7th. Note that this chord no longer has a 5th but we know from our charts that the 5th is optional in dominant chords.

D7

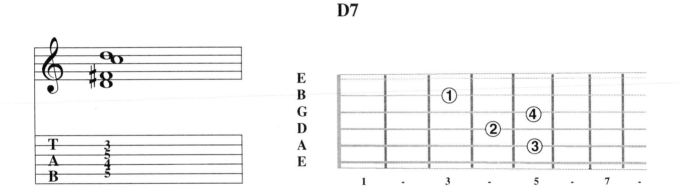

This dominant 7th has many close relatives. Raise the 5th three frets to a flat 7th and raise the 8th one fret to a flat 9th for a 7th flat 9th chord. This is another chord which sounds rather odd when played alone but it provides very nice tension and flavor when it is used in the right context. (See the next Playbreak)

D7♭9

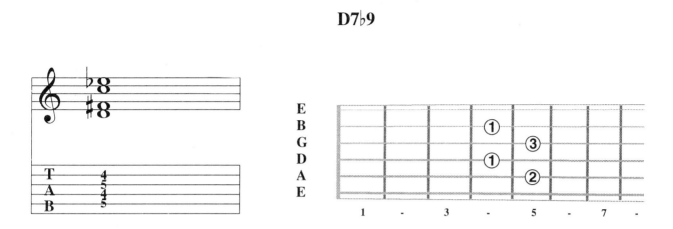

For a dominant 9th chord, raise the 5th two frets to a flat 7th and raise the 8th two frets to a 9th. This is a great blues chord, and you can use it as a tasty substitution for boring old 7th chords.

D9

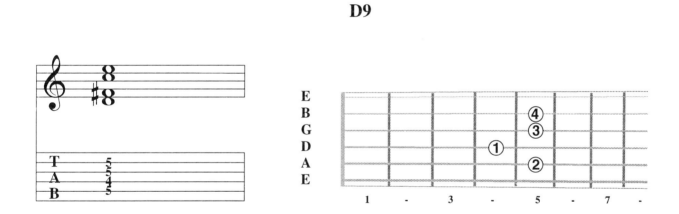

THE JIMI

Now we come to my personal favorite, the 7th sharp 9th chord. Remember *Purple Haze?* If you've heard that song you've heard this chord. I call this one the *JIMI.* This chord is a fascinating example of how new sounds creep into everyday usage, lose their strangeness and become "normal" to our ears. The 7#9 sound was only found as a passing chord in jazz until Hendrix used it in several much played songs. Before his common usage of this jarring chord it sounded odd on its own but our taste and ears have come to accept this "new" sound.

D7#9

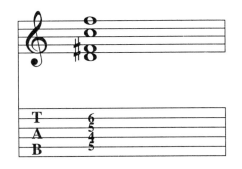
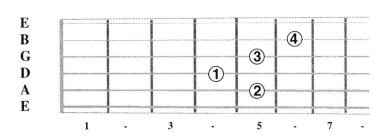

PLAYBREAK
Look Sharp or Be Flat

This little series gives a sense of how dominant chords can be substituted for each other. Listen as the movement of a single note within these dominant family chords adds richness and complexity to the progression.

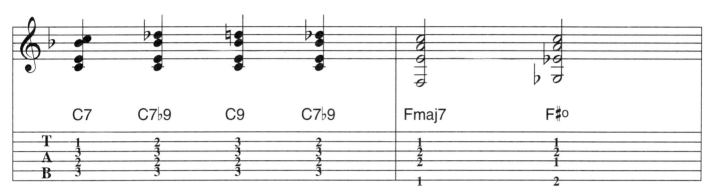

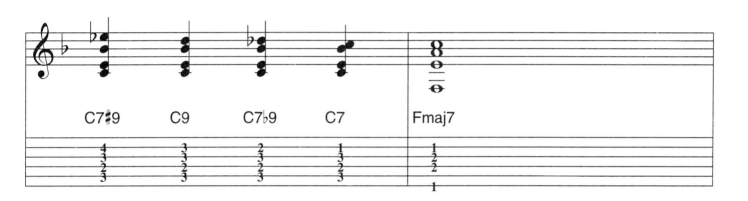

We can make a new minor family chord by keeping our 9th (raised from the 8th) and flat 7th (raised from the 5th) and lowering the 3rd. This is a minor 9th chord.

Dm9

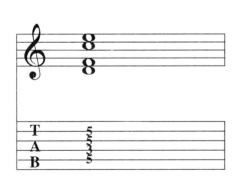

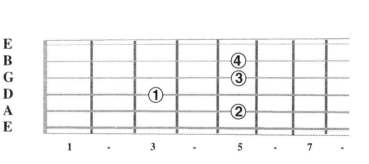

One more useful minor voicing can be made by starting with our minor 9th fingering and raising the 9th one fret. Remember, just as the 8th is another root or 1, the 9th is a 2nd. By raising the 2nd one fret, we get a flat 3rd. This chord has a sparse and very minor sound since it has not one but two minor 3rds.

Dm7

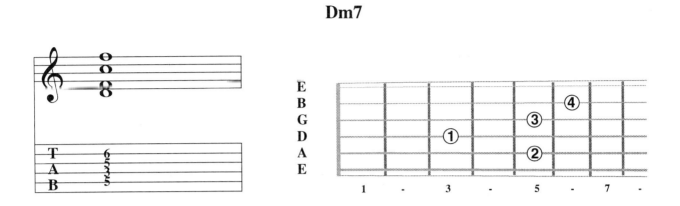

Finally let's alter the major by raising the 5th. This gives us an augmented chord. This is the first time we have raised the 5th of a chord without having a flatted 7th as well. This chord belongs to the Altered chord family.

D+(D♯5)

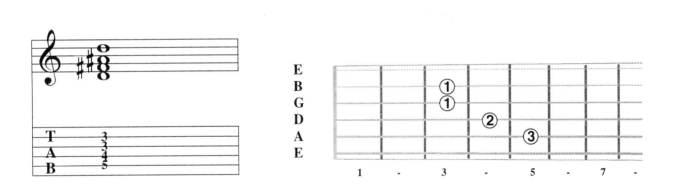

EXERCISES

1.) The root note for the C form chords is on the A string like the A forms. Here is a review of the notes on the A string. Write in the notes on the grid.

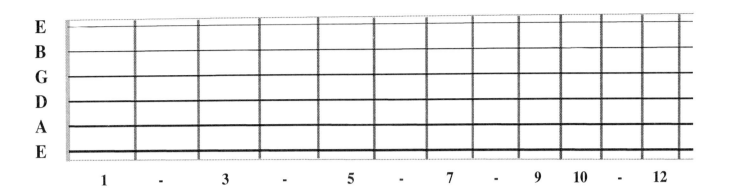

2.) Using the C forms from this chapter find the following chords: D♭ - E7♯9 - E7 - G9 - Cm9 - F6 - D♭7♭9 - Emaj9

3.) Find the following chords in three places using the E, A, and C forms: Gmaj7 - F7 - E♭6 -Dm7

CHAPTER SIX

MAKING CHORDS
FROM THE "D" MAJOR SHAPE

So far we've worked with chords that have their root notes on the E and A strings. Let's mess with the D major chord form. Below is the basic open D chord.

D

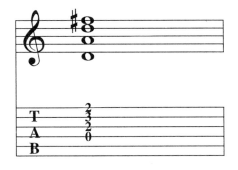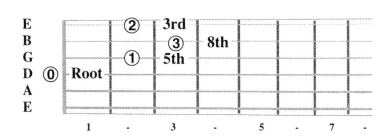

This should start to sound familiar by now. The D major shape can be moved anywhere on the fretboard without losing its majorness.

F

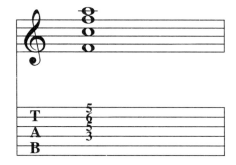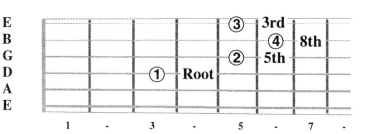

The major family includes lowering the 8th one fret to a 7th to make a major 7th chord.

Fmaj7

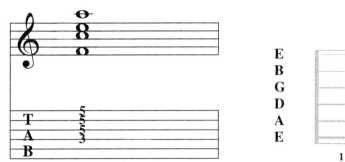 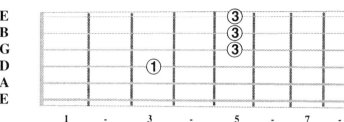

How about a major 6th? Lower the 8th on the B string three frets to a 6th and keep everything else.

F6

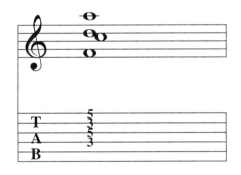 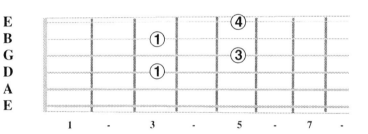

Lots of minor chords can be created from the D form. First for the plain old minor we lower the 3rd on the E string by one fret.

Fm

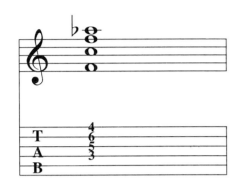 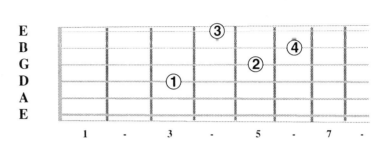

A minor chord with a major 7th added to it needs a flat 3rd to be minor and to add the major 7th, lower the 8th by one fret to a 7th. This is another example of a chord that is usually used in passing.

Fm/maj7

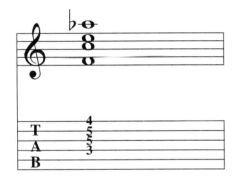 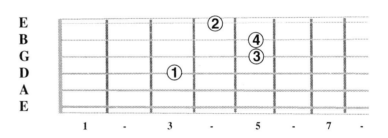

The minor 7th needs a flat 3rd, and the 8th on the B string is lowered by two frets to a flat 7th to make a very useful Fm7.

Fm7

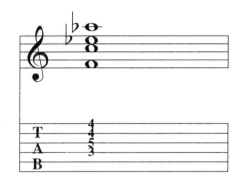
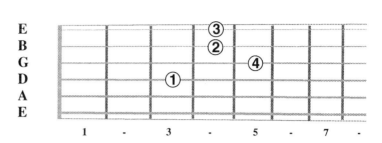

For a nice minor 6th just keep moving the flat 7th down. Remember the chord name tells all-the root is F-the minor tells us that the 3rd is flat-and we move the 8th from the original major chord down 3 frets to a 6th.

Fm6

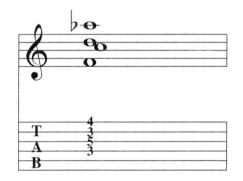
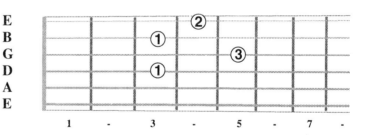

How about a dominant 7th? Only one change from the major shape. Lower only the 8th by two frets to a flat 7th.

F7

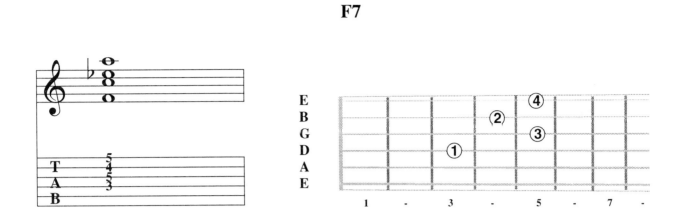

Let's make a few altered chords. First a suspended fourth needs to have the 3rd on the E string raised one fret to a 4th. When you play this one listen to the sense of unfinished business that this sound has.

Fsus4

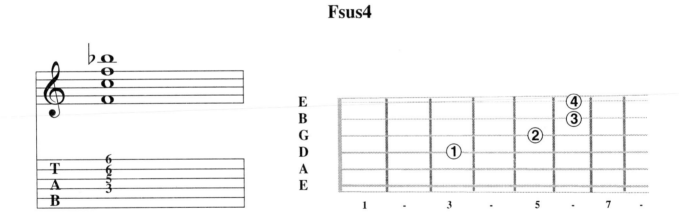

For a 7th suspended 4th, raise the 3rd one fret, and lower the 8th two frets to a flat 7th. The sound of this chord gives an even more unfinished feeling. Kind of like the Amen in a church hymn with out the "men" part. It leaves you feeling sort of um, well "suspended".

F7sus4

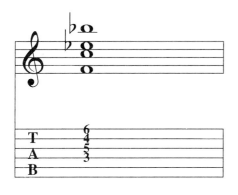
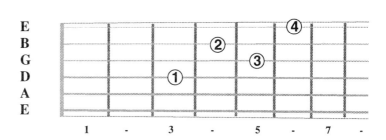

To make a minor 7th with a flat 5th or half diminished chord, lower the 3rd by one fret, lower the 8th by two frets, and lower the 5th by one fret.

Fm 7♭5 (Fø)

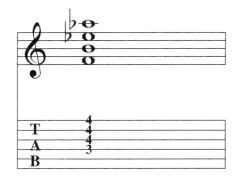
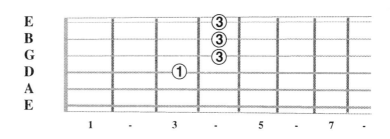

67

Finally for a full diminished chord , lower the 3rd one fret, lower the 8th three frets (to a double flat 7th), lower the 5th one fret.

Fø

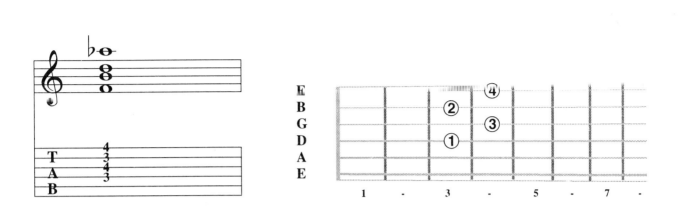

All of these shapes are of course moveable to any position on the fretboard but to really use them effectively, you must learn not only the shapes but also the root note names on the D string.

PLAYBREAK
Suspension Bridge

This little ditty uses our new D shapes to make a downward chord movement eventually move to a key one fret (one half step) higher each time we play the chord sequence.

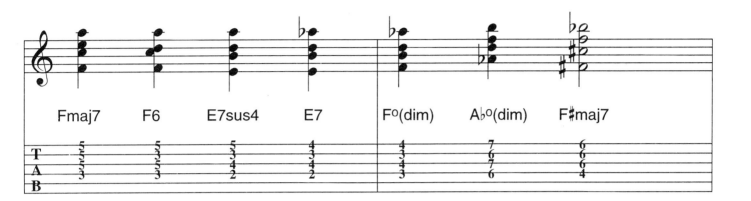

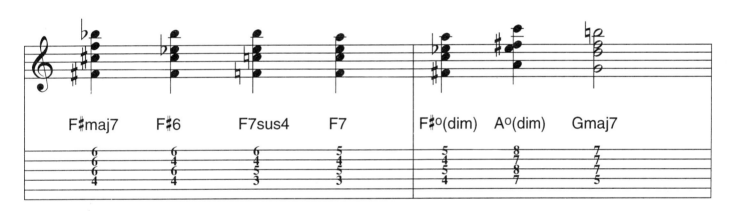

EXERCISES

Lets review the E and A strings by filling in the missing note names.

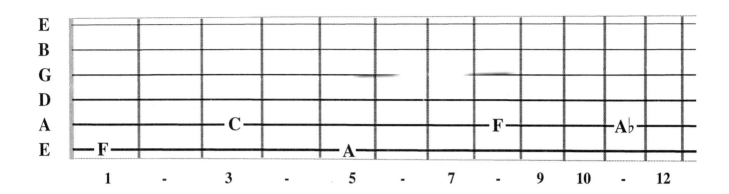

In order to use the D form chords in chapter six, we need to know the note names on the D string. Fill in the missing notes on the D string. Now look at the relationship between the E and D string.

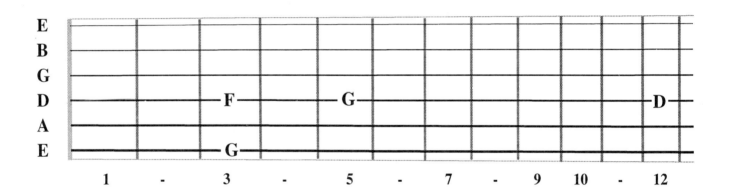

That's right! The D string two frets up is one octave higher than the low E. The rule is: two strings over—two frets up. A nice tool that works with the A and G strings as well.

CHAPTER SEVEN

ODDS, ENDS, SLASH CHORDS
SLICK TRICKS
and
BIZARRE COINCIDENCES

Below is the shape of an F major chord. In fact, if you look closely, it is the top 4 strings of the E major bar we examined earlier. It presents some great possibilities for creating new chord shapes.

F

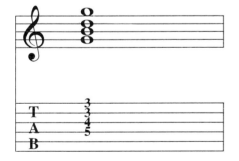

This shape is moveable to any place on the fretboard like this!

G

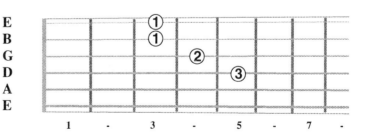

For a very useful major 7th, lower the 8th on the E string one fret to a 7th. Because of the voicing, this shape is great for arpeggios and sweep picking.

Gmaj7

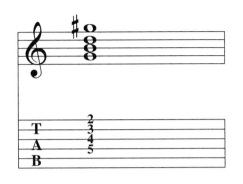

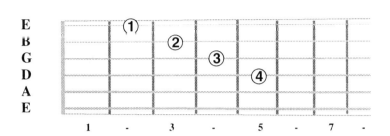

PLAYBREAK
Sweepin' Up

Sweep picking is a pick technique that works great with C and F shape chords. These two shapes work well because the order of the intervals is root, 3rd, 5th, 8th (or whatever you change the 8th to, in this case a major 7th). In measures 1 and 3, SWEEP your pick downward across the D and E♭ major 7th chords. In measures 2 and 4, SWEEP your pick upwards over the G and A♭ major 7th chords. As you cross each string, lift the finger holding the note slightly so that each note sounds separately. The effect is of a very fast series of single notes rather than a chord arpeggio.

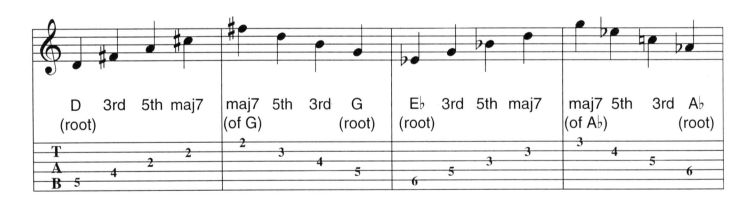

72

The next four chords are made from the F form and come as a set. The first is a minor made by lowering the 3rd in the F form by one fret.

Am

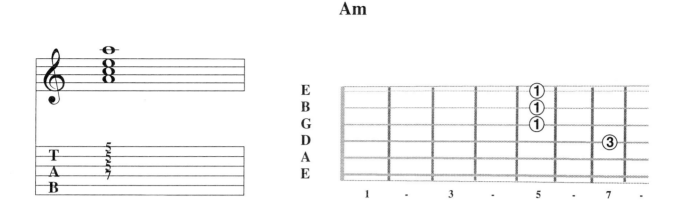

The next chord is an example of a slash chord. The top three notes are still A minor but there is a 7th in the lowest voice. It could be called a minor with a major 7th or A minor G# bass note and in fact we've seen it before in chapter 3 as a Gm/maj7 with the root (G) as the lowest note on the low E string.

Am/maj7 or Am/G#

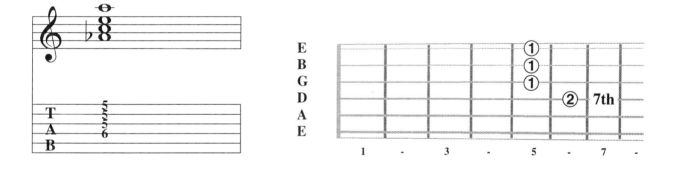

Next up is still an A minor 7th except, the lowest note is ***not*** an A. It is the flat 7th. The top three notes are still A minor. This chord can also be named as a slash chord.

Am7 or Am/G

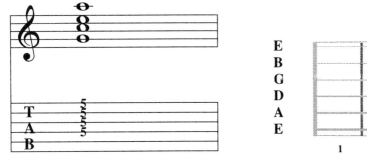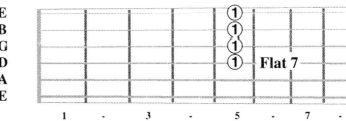

Finally lower the flat 7th to a 6th. Again we have two names, A minor 6th or A minor with an F♯ bass note

Am6 or Am/F♯

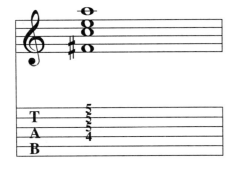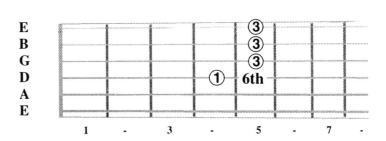

PLAYBREAK
Ladder to Valhalla

Here is a tidbit that may sound familiar. We'll walk the bass voice down just as we did with the inner voice in chapter 4.

SLASH AWAY

One more little tip on slash chords. They are often chords that you already know with a different bass note. For example, here is a normal open A chord:

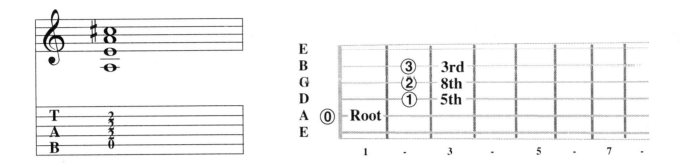

Okay, now suppose the symbol you see is A/C♯. Read this a an A chord with a C♯ as the bass note.

A/C♯

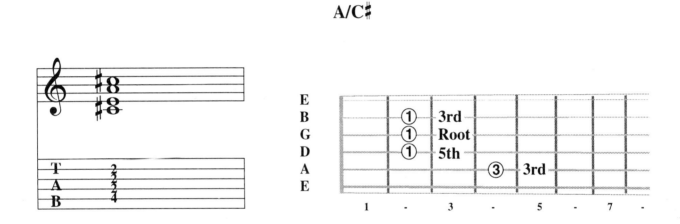

Looking at the chord above, we can see that it still has the root, 3rd, 5th and shape of an A major chord. But the original root has been replaced with a 3rd as the bass (lowest) note. This chord is also called a 1st inversion chord. A 2nd inversion would have the 5th as lowest note. Try to find one.

The chord below has the root, 3rd, and 5th of an A major chord as well but this time it has a B in the bass.

A/B

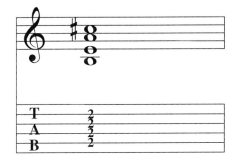 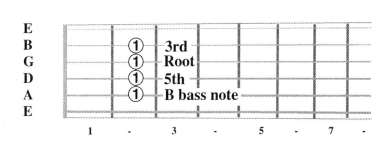

Bsus

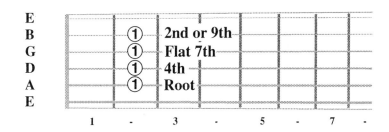

The chord above has two names. You can see that, from an A form point of view, it is an A chord with a B in the bass. But if we think of the B note as the root of the chord it is a B chord with a 4th, a flat 7th, and a 9th or 2nd. Both the 4th and the 2nd can be thought of as suspended. This chord is used extensively in jazz and is referred to as a *sus* chord.

This seems a good place to end this foolishness as it is a great example of the way you look at a chord determining how well you understand it. I know that if you work on the concepts and practice, this book will give you the tools to play effectively from lead sheets, charts and books. More importantly, I hope that it will help you to think about and have a better understanding of chords, and open new musical worlds to you.

WRAP IT UP, I'LL TAKE IT

If you follow the steps in this book for building new chords, you will now have the ability to look at virtually any lead sheet, fake book or sheet music that has guitar chord symbols and *figure out on your own how to play the chords.* Not only that, but you are not limited to one position for each chord. Many of the chord types, like major 7ths, can be played 4 or 5 different ways in different places on the neck.

Of course, the real test comes after you have figured out the right chord. It still takes a good deal of practice to change these chord shapes quickly and musically. By using different forms, you can usually find shapes that are very close together regardless of the chord changes.

SUBSTITUTE, SUBSTITUTE

My last bit of wisdom is as follows. The chord families are important. You can usually substitute chords within their families.

For example, if you see a D7, you can *usually* substitute another *dominant chord* like a D9 or D13. Likewise, if the symbol is C, you may usually substitute a Cmaj7, C6 or Cmaj9 (not C9, it's a dominant), and for an Fm, you could use an Fm9 or Fm7.

The melody line often will give you a clue for chord subs. If the chord is C7 and the melody at that point is an F note, it follows that since C to F is a 4th, you could play a C7sus4 and have an excellent substitution. There is however no substitute for a good ear. Remember that you need to listen very carefully to make sure the substitutions sound right. A good ear is not something that you are born with. If you *practice* and *listen,* you can develop a great ear for the right sounds. The last two Playbreaks will give you a taste of how the many chords we have learned will fit together. The next book in this series, *UNDERSTANDING CHORD PROGRESSIONS* gives insights and details of how chords and melodies fit together and interact.

Experiment with your own chord voicing. Have fun! Be musical! Good luck and may the force be with you!

PLAYBREAK
Bad Bad Blues

The 12 bar blues is a very common musical form in Jazz, Blues and Rock/pop. The one below is a sorta Jazz style blues. Some of the chords may take a bit of getting used to or they may sound just plain wrong to you! Play them and decide.

79

PLAYBREAK
Walk the Line

The bass notes in the first measure of this chord series walk upward to the same chord in inversion form (G/B) and on one fret farther to the first chord of the second measure (C). The chords in measure 2 just keep on walkin' in much the same pattern. This chord/bass line movement sounds very slick in a blues progression. Try the first measure as a substitute for the first measure of the last Playbreak ***Bad Bad Blues.*** The chords would be B♭13, Cm♯5, C♯dim, B♭/D.

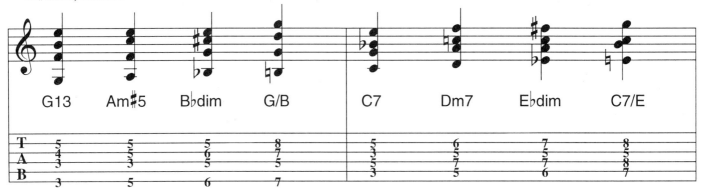

ABOUT THE AUTHOR

Bob Balsley began teaching guitar at the age of 15. He has continued performing, writing, recording and teaching for more than thirty years. He has played with many top performers, including Chuck Berry, Bobby Vinton, Holly Dunn, Roger Williams, Randy Brecker and Mickey Gilley and as this list would suggest he is skilled at many musical styles. He has performed in Guatemala, Tunisia, Netherlands and London. He has recorded as a solo artist and has been featured on many projects. He currently produces and records at his own studio in Green Bay Wisconsin.

He studied theory, performance and composition at College of Marin with S. Drummond Wolfe and received a B.A. from the University of Wisconsin-Green Bay. He has taught applied guitar and Guitar Ensemble at UW-Green Bay for the past seven years. He also teaches recording, audio engineering and MIDI at Northeastern Wisconsin Technical College. The UW-Green Bay Summer Guitar Camp that he founded in 1994 has attracted national media attention and continues to grow.

Bob is a sought-after clinician at schools and music stores as an Endorsing Artist for Heritage Washburn and Frye Guitars. His insightful articles have appeared in *Fingerstyle Guitar* magazine. His philosophy stresses music as a life-long activity that enriches the individual and the community.